Dedication

To my wife, Joyce, who continually inspires me to strive for bigger and greater accomplishments. She is my inspiration, my anchor and my love.

Table of Contents

Introduction

In business, you face an imminent threat. It will determine the survival of your business. In fact, it's already having a negative impact on your business. The mere reason you have to work as hard as you do to get the meager results you're getting tells me all I need to know. And because of it, you face extinction.

You are wrestling with obscurity. Obscurity is the great business killer for business. Traditionally it has been argued that the reason for most, if not all business failure, is because of the lack of cash flow. While I don't disagree that cash flow is king and will make or break your business, that's just the outward appearance and result of what obscurity has done to your business.

According to the Merriam-Webster Dictionary, the definition of obscurity is:

- The state of being unknown or forgotten
- Something that is difficult to understand
- The quality of being difficult to understand

You've been wrestling with obscurity for quite a while. You've poured a tremendous amount of money into advertising and, while it's worked to a certain degree, your business hasn't gained the traction you have been looking for. To eliminate obscurity, you will need to make a choice: Poor a ton of more money into your advertising budget or find a better way to deal with your obscurity.

Given how well that ad budget has worked in the past, isn't it time we look at some better options?

Why You are Obscure

Let's face it: Unless you've come up with the better mouse trap, you're faced with a lot of competition. Everyone is fighting for the same customer. And, as a result, this creates a lot of market "noise" that distracts the customer. Your business is drowning in the noise, unable to reach the right customer at the right time.

The traditional solution has been to create a better, more effective, even sexier marketing campaign to attempt to capture the attention of the target audience. This is fine if you are Coca-Cola, AT&T, Ford, or any number of Fortune 500 companies with deep advertising budgets. Advertising can work wonders for breaking through the obscurity barrier, but it requires a huge investment and a consistently high volume of messages. And even then advertising tends to be an intrusive message that falls on more deaf ears than we'd prefer.

At it's best, advertising is just a shot over the bow with a shotgun. Out of all the pellets in the casing, one may hit it's intended target. Most miss badly. Those who view the advertising view it as a distraction, even annoying. Is it any wonder that people record their favorite TV programs so they can fast forward through the commercials? Or that they subscribe Sirrius/XM radio in order to eliminate the advertising during their commute to and from work?

What Can You Do?

You have two options to take. Option One is that you can choose to do nothing. Given your initial options of doing nothing more or less than what you've done

6

already or investing hundreds of thousands of dollars into an advertising campaign that is a gamble at best, you're likely to choose the path of least resistance.

To this point, if you're still misleading yourself, you are having limited results. You're getting by. After all, it takes years, sometimes decades to grow a hugely successful business, right?

Too many businesses settle to continue to operate in mediocrity. They take what business comes. They might make an occasional attempt at a marketing strategy, but it's poorly done and lacks the penetration to have a decent impact.

At the end of the day, the decision is made to continue to conduct business as usual.

The second option is to choose to dominate your space and blow obscurity out of the water! When you choose this option, you make your mark in the sand and let the world know that you are here, you exist and you intend to dominate the market you operate in. It sends a message to your competition that you intend to take business away from them and they can either chose to match you or let their business suffer the consequences.

In the end, it is the business that chooses to eliminate obscurity who wins. They begin to take market share and win deal after deal. Their reputation begins to precede them, actually bringing referrals to them without even having to ask. To their competition, it begins to appear that you're everywhere. It's almost like you've hired a small army of sales professionals to get the message out and that you're conducting some type of covert marketing operation.

Instead you're simply choosing to eliminate obscurity and become the champion of your space!

The purpose of this book is to provide both business owners and sales professionals with a clear and definitive way to explode on to the scene and shift from being obscure to being the dominant name in your market space.

Dominating your space is not for the faint of heart, however. It takes work and it takes intestinal fortitude to commit to doing what it will require to truly dominate your market. Keep reading and, more importantly, choose to take action of the ideas you will read about and you will be on your path to dominating your market space.

Who Is This Book For?

This book is intended for anyone who desires to be known as the best and only real, viable option in the industry they operate in. To identify and implement a strategy to blow obscurity out of the water, this must become your driving obsession every day. This book will provide you with concrete, proven ideas and strategies to make obscurity in your business an endangered species.

Learn to Enhance the Numbers Game

Business owners and sales professionals are challenged by the adverse impact of obscurity every day. As a result, they literally have to work tirelessly every day just for the opportunity to meet a potential client for the very first time. They play the numbers game and find they have to reach ten possible clients – at the very least - in order to get just one to agree to a meeting.

What if, instead, your clients eagerly introduced you to potential new business?

What would it be like if your phone rang and it was a prospective client asking to meet so you can help them address their challenges? More importantly, what if you are their first and only call and they don't expect to have to contact anyone else?

What if each day is less work and more fun as you spend your time solving problems instead of begging and pleading for prospects?

And what if you were making 10 times more income than you ever dreamed because you simply had the business coming to you?

This is what happens when you dominate your market. But it requires a deep and abiding commitment from you. It means you must commit to creating the drive and the will to generate the level of activity to literally annihilate obscurity. You will need to reach down deep and commit to making it happen.

If dominating your market space appeals to you, then you are holding the right source to put you on the right path to success. The strategies contained in this book will shift you from mediocrity to the dominant force in your local market space, if not beyond. It will require effort on your part. It will take persistence and an abiding commitment. It will even take some serious intestinal fortitude to push through the noise and naysayers to make it happen. But it works. And isn't it time you began to start getting properly rewarded for your efforts? Isn't it time that everyone in your market space knows who you are and that everyone else is simply second best?

I challenge you to press forward and begin to make a significant difference in your business and in your life.

Section One

Why You Must Choose Dominating Instead of Competing

Chapter One

Compete or Dominate

"You can dominate a game if you dominate on the line...We're just going to have to go out there and work hard and blow people off the ball, and let our runners do what they do best."
--Miles Davis

"Identify your niche and dominate it. And when I say dominate, I just mean work harder than anyone else could possibly work at it."
--Nate Parker

Up to this point, you've been competing. You're one of many in your market space competing for market share, for customers, for sales and revenue. After all, competing for business is what it's all about, isn't it? Competition, as the lie goes, is good for business. But I have to ask: Do you really like competing? Is it really good for you?

It is argued that competition is good for consumers because, in theory, it provides them choices. Theoretically, it keeps the costs down. In reality, the consumer suffers because the businesses that are competing have to sacrifice profits to reinvest into the company and/or quality suffers in order to keep costs down. Jobs are reduced in order to manage the cost of operation. And, as a result, the quality of customer service is far less than it should be.

Competition certainly is not good for individual businesses. In the business world, when we choose to compete rather than completely dominate, we give other businesses hope. Hope is what is given when other companies think they are on the same playing field as you. When just a glimmer of hope is provided, it enables others to believe they can beat you.

In short, every time you view someone else as your competitor, you…

- Make them credible
- Allow them to see themselves as a suitable alternative
- Give them space IN your space
- You subconsciously agree to play fair and play by the "agreed upon" rules of engagement

It is just like athletics. A sports team's desire and ultimate goal is to dominate their opponent. They watch film. They practice every conceivable situation that might occur in the game. They prepare for every potential option and prepare so their actions become second nature. Sports teams that take this approach are those we refer to as "dynasties." Whether it's the Yankees, the Los Angeles Lakers, the Miami Heat, the New England Patriots or the Crimson Tide of Alabama, a dynasty occurs when there is a complete commitment to viewing victory and success as the only option.

In sports, competition is necessary. There must be two opponents and a scoreboard in order to understand who wins and who loses. Without competition, fans refuse to watch and the value of professional sports is eliminated. There must be a winner and a loser.

At the same time, as the late Al Davis of the Oakland Raiders says, "You don't adjust. You just dominate." Even though these teams need competitors, their goal is complete domination and be the team everyone else wants to become.

What it Takes to Dominate

To dominate requires unwavering commitment from you to:

- *Commit to taking massive action.*

  Taking massive action means you will establish a pace and put forth an effort that is unmatched by anyone else in your market space. This is why domination is not for the faint of heart. If you're not prepared to take massive action consistently, don't pretend to want to dominate.

- *Commit to doing what everyone else won't do.*

  There are specific things your competitors won't do or aren't doing to drive business growth. To dominate, you must be prepared to do what they won't do.

- *A complete commitment to dominate your space.*

Every time someone wins and you lose, it takes money out of your pocket and away from your company. Every time you lose, your family loses and your company loses. Most of all, your customer loses. They miss out on the quality service and great products you provide and they miss out on having you as part of the package.

**"Number one, cash is king...
number two, communicate...
number three, buy or bury the competition."**

--Jack Welch

Examples of Domination

In the '60s and '70s, Xerox was THE company when it came to copying documents. Not only did they own the patents for xerography, but they were everywhere. For nearly three decades, no one asked to get something copied; instead they'd ask, "Would you Xerox that for me?" While today there are many competitors in the same industry, Xerox is still considered by many to be the go-to-brand for printing and they do so while spending a much higher price.

In the '90s, at the height of the dot.com bubble, search engines were fighting for awareness. They each wanted to become the "go-to" source for finding information of any kind on the internet. Today, Google completely dominates this market. With a 64.1% market share, it overshadows the other two "competitors" by a large gap. In second is Yahoo with 18% and Microsoft's Bing at 13.6%. Together, all three control 98.5% of the search engine market. But Google comes to win when it pertains to the search engine market.

When it comes to soft drinks, everyone has their preference but when asked, it's far easier to say, "I'll have a Coke." It's at the tip of the tongue for good reason unless you're in the Carolinas of the United States. In the soft drink market, Coca-Cola owns the lion's share at 41.2% while PepsiCo is just behind with 33.6%. While this appears to be a slender difference, when compared in dollars, the gap is considerably wider.

Consider the world of tire manufacturing. In this arena, there are a number of manufacturers world-wide, but one stands out. Goodyear owns the market with 39% of the market share followed by Michelin at 28.2%. Goodyear not only leads the pack but they dominate as well.

Lastly, let's look at the major household appliance manufacturers. In this competitive industry, it would be easy to assume that there are a number of key players in the mix, but instead, four manufacturers together own 90% of the market.

- Whirlpool   43.8%
- AB Electrolux   20.7%
- General Electric   17.1%
- LG Electronics   9.2%

Whirlpool, at 43.8%, has almost as much market share as the next three combined. According to IBISWorld, Inc., "The industry is expected to become even more concentrated in the next five years. Firms such as Whirlpool and Electrolux are expected to acquire more companies, further reducing the number of enterprises. These acquisitions will add to the companies' economies of scale, lowering production costs and enabling firms to broaden their product ranges. The industry is expected to grow 2.2% in 2012 to $17.6 billion."[1]

In each of these examples, these industry leaders have chosen to dominate their space. While they are not alone in their market space, they clearly have a distinct advantage in terms of market awareness and in market valuation. A company like Whirlpool isn't content with just being the dominant player. Instead they are consistently looking for additional partners to grow their business and increase their effectiveness in the market.

Just like each of these, you must seek to be the dominant player in your industry. Anything less is settling to be a competitor. And competitors get left in the dust.

---

[1] Web Source:
http://www.themarketworks.org/sites/default/files/uploads/charts/Highly -Concentrated-Industries.pdf - Highly Concentrated: Companies That Dominate Their Industries by IBISWorld, Inc., February 2012

Chapter Two

Be Part of the Top 1%

"The best way to predict the future is to create it."
--Peter Drucker

"I am the greatest, I said that even before I knew I was."
--Muhammad Ali

The Pareto Principle is one of the most famous economic principles. It states that 20% of something creates 80% of the results. In sales, this means that 20% of your activities will generate 80% of your results; 20% of your customers will account for 80% of your revenue; and 80% of your company's business will be generated by 20% of your reps. It is an invaluable principle and, for the purposes of dominating your market, is utterly out of place.

While you may be satisfied with joining the ranks of the top 20% of your company or the top 20% of your industry, I want to challenge you to set your sights higher. I want you to see yourself attaining the top 1% of the top 20%.

The Top 1% Utterly Dominate

Let's look at the wealthiest top 1% of people in the United States and compare them with everyone else. For illustration, here is a chart designed by Professor G.

William Domhoff in his online article, "Wealth, Income and Power" for his web, Who Rules America.

Income, Net Worth and Financial Worth in the US[2]

Wealth or Income Class	Mean Household Income	Mean Household Net Worth	Mean Household Financial (non-home) Wealth
Top 1 Percent	$1,318,200	$16,439,400	$15,171,600
Top 20 Percent	$226,200	$2,061,600	$1,719,800
60th – 80th Percentile	$72,000	$216,900	$100,700
40th – 60th Percentile	$41,700	$61,000	$12,200
Bottom 40 Percent	$17,300	<$10,600>	<$14,800>

While this information was intended for something much different, what I want to point out is very much straight to the point. Notice the difference between the top 1% and the top 20%. The top 1% earns nearly $1.1 million a year more in household income. Worse, those in the top 20% are considered just above the ranks of the middle class by $1,200.

Let's be honest: Where do you want to be…really?

What kind of difference can you make in the world with an extra $1.1 million?

---

[2] Web Source: http://www2.ucsc.edu/whorulesamerica/power/wealth.html, Wealth, Income, and Power by G. William Domhoff, February 2013.

What can you and your family accomplish with a net worth that is $12 million more than those in the top 20%?

In order to become part of the top 1%, you must learn to completely dominate your market. It's not enough to compete at a very high level. It's not enough to say you work hard and keep your nose to the proverbial grind stone. For many reading this book, you've been doing just that – keeping your nose to the grind stone; working hard; coming in early and staying late. How's that working for you? To me, you're operating like the rest of the top 20%. You're slave to old traditions and outmoded principles. There was a day and time when that was enough and you could accomplish great things, but those days are gone. You just need to get next to it.

To elevate your experience, you need to raise the stakes in the game of life. You need to raise your personal expectations and create the type of work ethic that will elevate you to the top 1%.

The Middle Class is a Vanishing Act

The Middle Class, as an economic reality, is a vanishing act. For decades, the Middle Class represented a social setting between the Upper Class and the Lower/Impoverished Class. But as the world's economy has changed as a result of the Great Recession of 2008, the socio-economic landscape has changed.

Please don't get me wrong; I'm not arguing against the values of the Middle Class. It is a proud, hard working class of people. I, for one, am part of this classification, albeit part of the upper middle class. What I am arguing for is a change in our economic outlook. The financial wealth of the world is changing hands and the balance of power, especially in the United States, is shifting. It is imperative that we shift our focus to becoming part of the top 1% in order to outlast the final vestiges of what is left of the Middle Class.

A Social Argument for Dominating

If we've learned anything from Bill Gates over the past few decades it is this: Being part of the top 1% can create tremendous change in our world for the better. Of course it takes having the character and outlook that drives Bill and his wife, Melinda, but their tireless work of providing effective health care and clean drinking water for impoverished countries is an example of how you and I can change our world.

The following is from a letter Bill and Melinda Gates explaining their philosophy behind their philanthropic efforts:

Our friend and co-trustee Warren Buffett once gave us some great advice about philanthropy: "Don't just go for safe projects," he said. "Take on the really tough problems."

We couldn't agree more. Our foundation is teaming up with partners around the world to take on some tough challenges: extreme poverty and poor health in developing countries, and the failures of America's education system. We focus on only a few issues because we think that's the best way to have great impact, and we focus on these issues in particular because we think they are the biggest barriers that prevent people from making the most of their lives.

For each issue we work on, we fund innovative ideas that could help remove these barriers: new techniques to help farmers in developing countries grow more food and earn more money; new tools to prevent and treat deadly diseases; new methods to help students and teachers in the classroom. Some of the projects we fund will fail. We not only accept that, we expect it— because we think an essential role of philanthropy is to make bets on promising solutions that governments and businesses can't afford to make. As we learn which bets pay off, we have to adjust our strategies and share the results so everyone can benefit.

We're both optimists. We believe by doing these things—

focusing on a few big goals and working with our partners on innovative solutions—we can help every person get the chance to live a healthy, productive life.

Through their foundation, Bill and Melinda Gates hope to leave the world a much better place by tackling some of the world's most pressing problems. This is what happens when those in the top 1% leverage their resources to make a difference. It's also what can happen when you and I become part of the top 1%. It enables us to make a difference.

Are you going to settle? Are you so comfortable in your traditional middle class mindset that you're willing to let the foundation that supports you crumble away? That's what has and continues to happen to the old reality. The time has come for a new focus, a new tradition. The time has come for real leaders to step up from among the ranks of what's left of the middle class and help make a difference in the outcome of our world. I've already shifted in that direction; will you join me?

Chapter Three

Take Massive Action

"The path to success is to take massive, determined action."

--Tony Robbins

"Infuse your life with action. Don't wait for it to happen. Make it happen. Make your own future. Make your own hope. Make your own love. And whatever your beliefs, honor your creator, not by passively waiting for grace to come down from upon high, but by doing what you can to make grace happen... yourself, right now, right down here on Earth."

--Bradley Whitford

What sets Steve Jobs, Bill Gates and Warren Buffett apart from you and me? What's the distinguishing difference? Yes, they are incredibly wealthy, but set that aside. What truly makes the difference?

What about Mark Cuban, Larry Page, Mary Barra or Sergey Brin? What makes the difference between them and you?

The critical difference between each of these people and you is a simple element. It is an element that you and I are very capable of utilizing but, far too often, we fail to do so. In fact, most of the time we choose not to use it because of our own fear. Our fear has trapped us, immobilizing us to the extent that we're unwilling or unable to take the necessary risks. It is this very fear that separates the highly successful from the wannabes.

The difference is in their desire and commitment to consistently taking massive action to accomplish their goals. In the lives of each of the individuals I just mention, they have consistently chosen to take massive action to make their dreams a reality and create a new future for themselves and their families. And it is, as Tony Robbins is famous for saying, "in your moments of decision that your destiny is shaped."

Consider Mary Barra, the first woman to ever head a Big 8 automaker. As the CEO of General Motors, she has stepped into a difficult time in the life of GM, facing 30 million auto recalls, and yet remains poised and confident. In fact, she continues to drive GM into the future with technology that will change the future of driving around the world with the announcement of the 2017 Cadillac that will literally be able to drive itself on the highway.

Mary Barra wasn't simply handed the reins to GM. She has worked tirelessly throughout her career to position herself for this ultimate job in the auto industry. Leading the world's largest auto maker, regardless of gender, is a daunting task, but as a woman especially, it's a challenge given the glass ceiling in the auto industry for women.

Starting with GM in 1980 as a co-op student from Kettering University, Mary has consistently worked to reach new goals and challenges. During her career at GM, she has worked as the plant manager at the Detroit Hamtramck Assembly Plant; executive director of Competitive Operations Engineering; and general director of Internal Communications for GM North America. And every step of the way, she faced the challenge of being a woman in what is traditionally a male-dominated workplace environment.

And today, at the age of 53, Mary Barra is considered one of the world's most powerful women.

Sergey Brin, co-founder with Larry Page of Google in 1998, started life in Moscow, Russia. His father was a mathematics economist and Sergey's mother worked as a researcher for NASA's Goddard Space Flight Center. After years of struggling with the intrusive and obvious limitations placed on Russian Jews, Sergey's father decided to relocate the family to the United States when Sergey was six years old.

In spite of the dramatic impact of such a significant relocation from Russia to the US, Sergey pursued his love of mathematics and computer science. He attended and graduated from the University of Maryland in 1993 with a Bachelors of Science degree.

It was at the University of Maryland that he met Larry Page and they struck up a friendship through their common interest in computer science. Page wanted to explore the mathematical properties of the World Wide Web and found Sergey to be interested as well.

Starting with a project called "BackRub," they developed a web crawler to explore the internet using Stanford University's home page. Their exploration helped them discover that a search engine based on PageRank would provide much more extensive results than those other search engines used.

After months of testing on Stanford's website, they registered the domain "google.com" in 1997. Then, in 1998, they incorporated and began operating out of a friend's garage in Menlo Park, California.

Today, Google is a power house transforming the way information is disseminated across the globe as well as how business gets done. Marketing depends so much on how Google views each search engine optimization (SEO) approach, that they bow to the great power in order to be recognized early and often on every Google search.

Not only has Google been handsomely rewarded in terms of its great wealth, but Google now finds itself in the stratosphere among great names such as Xerox and Kleenex. It is a brand that people associate with internet search so much that they don't refer to an internet search; instead they "Google it."

Succeeding at a high level requires massive action. While many prefer to simply label success stories as "lucky," I have found that, in reality, it's far more than just being lucky. It's like what

Samuel Goldwyn says, "The harder I work, the luckier I get." The more action you take, the "luckier" you will get.

Massive Action vs Life

Doesn't it seem that just as you really get into a groove, something happens? You get sick. Your kids get sick. The car breaks down or has a flat tire. A significant snow storm hits your community and everything shuts down. Regardless what happens, the bottom line is this: Life happens.

This is why taking massive action is so important. When you take massive action, it tends to compensate for the wrinkles life sends your way. While it doesn't eliminate the problems, it provides you with considerable cushion to deal with the challenges. Instead of allowing "life" to dictate or make a difference in your outcomes, leveraging massive action positions you to compensate even the slightest hiccup.

Average People Don't Take Massive Action

The primary reason that people like Sergey Brin and Bill Gates are the exception rather than the rule is that too many people act in an average way. They fail to take massive action and choose, instead, to take normal levels of action and, as a result, they get sub-par results.

Average action is the most deadly types of action because it lulls you into a fall sense of security. You think everything is fine because you're getting similar results compared to the rest of the group. But this is when everything tends to collapse around you. You walk out to your car to head to work and you have a flat tire. You head to your meeting to close the big account you've been working on for months and they call to say they've had to postpone the decision until the first of the year. Kids get sick. The country experiences a recession. A major US landmark is destroyed. Think of all of the life experiences we have faced since 2000. Each of these, while they have huge impacts on our lives, can be offset when we've invested massive action into our lives.

Average action gets you average results unless something goes wrong. And something always goes wrong. It's Murphy's Law: If something is going to go wrong, it will and it will happen to you. This is why average action is so dangerous. It gives you a false sense of security and then – boom – you're in a deep hole.

Massive action creates such a wave of momentum that when life happens, you're prepared to overcome any distraction and delay that occurs. Taking massive action enables you to create a powerful pipeline of business opportunities that, when one deal falls through, it's not the end of the world. And that's really the truth serum that tells you whether you've been operating with massive action or average action. If one deal makes or breaks you for the month, you've been relying far too much on average action!

Don't Listen to the Detractors

Champions who take massive action will always have their detractors. The detractors are those who are put off by your level of massive action and the results you're achieving. In my book, Roar Like You Mean It!, I discuss the hyenas we have to deal with when we take massive action and start getting amazing results. They begin to nip at your heels. They gang up on you, challenging the "sanity" for putting so much effort in. And then, when all else fails, they paint you as having the "best territory" or the "golden favorite" of the boss. You get ridiculed and stigmatized by the hyenas. Why? Your massive action and consequential success makes them look bad.

The crowd never appreciates the individual who takes massive action because it makes them feel uncomfortable. This is why they are stuck in the average circle. They fear the level of action success really requires, so they convince themselves – and others – that massive action is ludicrous and unnecessary. After all, they don't want to "burn out."

Burn out happens to those who have impotent goals and begin to experience the negative consequences of life. When individuals take average action and then fail to achieve their weak, impotent goals because of one distraction or another, it always is exposed and intensely magnified by the individual who is taking massive action and getting massive results. It makes them feel overwhelmed and their argument to themselves and others is that they're just getting burned out. We need to call "BS" when we see it.

Average people whine and they don't need to be listened to.

Start Taking Massive Action Today

The rest of this book is dedicated to showing you a different way. These strategies take you down a different path that will lead to extraordinary growth and success. They will empower you to dominate your market and reduce your competitors to after-thoughts.

But let's be clear: Dominating your market isn't going to happen if you simply keep doing the same things you've always done. And it's not going to happen if you continue to play by the traditional rules of the rest of the world. You will hear, "That's now how we've done this before." Simply nod and walk on. You need to break out and rise above the mediocre sales population.

Taking massive action and starting to do so today will put you in distinct company. Steve Jobs and Bill Gates didn't get to where they are at by taking average levels of action. Sergey Brin, Larry Page and Mary Barra didn't rise the ranks of giants by taking average action. Each of these people took bold, massive amounts of action and created incredible lives for themselves. And, in doing so, they have had a transformative effect on countless others, even the globe. Whether it's saving the world's largest automobile manufacturer from disaster or creating technology that transforms the way the world operates, it takes massive action to make a difference at that scale.

I know. You're not Sergey Brin or Steve Jobs. You are *"state your name"* and you're about to change the world you live and operate in by taking massive action. Whether your action changes the world at large or simply changes the part of the world in which you operate doesn't really matter. What matters is what impact it has on your life and the lives of those who matter most to you.

Step out of the shadows of the average and join me. Massive action is like body surfing. It's exhilarating when you catch the wave. Sometimes you'll bounce around and crash, but it's momentary. You just get up and catch the next wave. Another big wave is coming; will you be on it?

Section Two

Skills & Actions for Dominating Your Market

Chapter Four

No More White Space

"My wife's jealousy is getting ridiculous. The other day she looked at my calendar and wanted to know who May was."

--Rodney Dangerfield

If you want to identify who is serious about dominating their market, simply ask to see their calendar for the next two weeks. Viewing someone's calendar is like the looking at the vital signs of someone in the hospital; either you're improving and getting healthy or you're on life support. A white, empty calendar is the equivalent of someone on life support – assuming their career is still alive at all.

Your calendar, believe it or not, is what will dictate your ability to dominate, let alone succeed at any level. When your calendar reflects a substantial amount of white space – meaning far too few appointments and key sales activities – it means you're in for a very bumpy ride. In fact, you really should be getting your resume in order.

Too many sales people have far too much white space meaning that their time is open, flexible and unaccounted for. This unaccounted-for time is costly. It's time not scheduled in front of a client or a potential client.

It's time that, left unplanned, will disappear and will never be seen again.

In every work week, there are forty hours typically available to the average person. In a study done by Pace Productivity, here is how the average sales person spends their day:

**TYPICAL SALES REP
% OF WEEKLY HOURS**

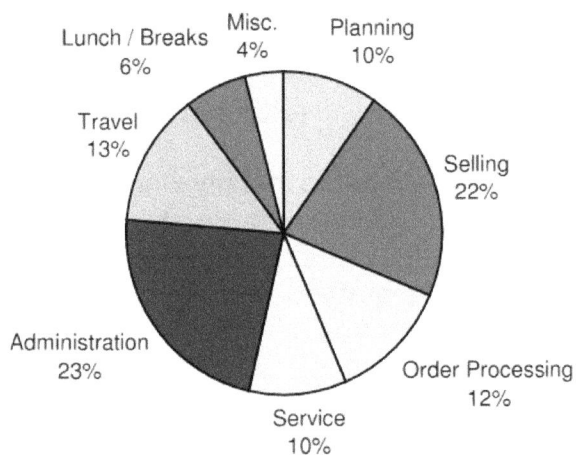

The primary reason a sales person has a job **_is to close business_** and yet only 22% of their day is spent actually selling. On the other hand, 78% of their day is spent doing the work that doesn't get them paid including 23% of time spent on administrative tasks, 12% on order processing, and 10% each on service and planning.

During a typical day, this means a sales person spends less than two hours in front of a client or future client. Two hours? That means this "sales professional" is spending less than ten hours a week doing <u>what they</u>

get paid to do while over 30 hours a week are spent doing "busy" work.

Don't get me wrong. I understand that there are a lot of demands on the time and for the attention of every sales professional. But what concerns me the most is that if a sales professional truly wants to dominate he or her market, why are they spending 78% of their time doing what someone else could be doing for them?

The reason the majority of sales professionals have white space on their calendar is because of this focus on the 78% of unproductive, non-revenue producing activities. What would happen if they shifted to 50%? What if you personally shifted your focus so that 70% or more of your calendar was focused on revenue production? A shift from 22% to 70% isn't just a 48% improvement in your results; instead it can have a 500% or more improvement in your actual results.

Reassign Non-Revenue Tasks

While your company may not hire a personal assistant to help you with your busy work, there isn't anything to prevent you from hiring a virtual assistant – from your own country or from abroad – to help you accomplish more.

What can you assign to a virtual assistant? Here are a few ideas:

- Bookkeeping
- Online Research
- Database entries
- Data presentations
- Managing email
- Social tasks

- Travel Research
- Scheduling
- Chasing business
- Industry knowledge prep

What about the cost of hiring a virtual assistant? It depends on where they are based.

- In the United States: $15 to $65 per hour depending on the work
- In India: $6.98 per hour

Just like hiring anyone "live" and in person, you can interview and select the viritual assistant you want. Just because they are virtual doesn't mean you just get stuck with any schlep that sits at the desk.

Best of all, while this is a cost of doing business, it also means there are tax incentives available to you as a result as long as you follow a few rules:

- No benefits are provided other than pay (no insurance or retirement benefits);
- An independent contractor (virtual assistant) typically works on a project basis, whereas an employee works under a long-term contract;
- An independent contractor (virtual assistant) typically sets their own schedule, uses their own tools and equipment and does the job with minimal supervision.

- You provide them with a form 1099 by January 31 to every independent contractor you paid at least $600 to in the previous calendar year.

I'm not an accountant nor do I play one on TV, so I recommend that you discuss this with a certified professional to see what the tax advantages would be as they pertain directly to you. But, in the end, I think you'll be pleased with the outcome.

What would happen if...?

Consider what will happen if you eliminate most, if not all, of the white space on your calendar. Instead of white space, imagine having lots of scheduled appointments and personal visits set up with existing clients and future clients.

If you fall into the category of "average sales professional" and face-to-face sales calls only account for 22% or less of your time (be honest with yourself!), then you really need to explore what the outcome would look like if you maximized your available time. What will happen if you truly devoted yourself, 70% to 80% of the time, to real selling opportunities?

I think we both know the answer to this.

Now stop imagining and make it happen!

Chapter Five

Credibility Matters

"The more you are willing to accept responsibility for your actions, the more credibility you will have."

--Brian Koslow

"In the end, you make your reputation and you have your success based upon credibility and being able to provide people who are really hungry for information what they want."

--Brit Hume

To succeed in business and in life, you must first start with your credibility. If you lack credibility, your work is 1,000 times more difficult. If you have immense credibility, your reputation precedes you. If you fail to recognize the importance of credibility, you do so at your own peril and you have no one to blame but yourself.

Merriam-Webster Dictionary defines credibility as:

- *The quality of being believed or accepted as true, real or honest*
- *The quality or power of inspiring belief*
- *Capacity for belief*

It's been said that "credibility is like virginity. Once you lose it, you can't get it back." In sales, you start out with diminished credibility due to the actions of unscrupulous sales people who went before you. Unfortunately, fair or not, sales people have borne the weight of the misdeeds of those who have gone before us. Their underhanded way of doing business, their fabrication of detail instead of a discourse based on fact, their "one night stand" approach to doing business have all conspired to do significant damage to the sales profession as a whole. As a result, simply being in the profession of sales makes you guilty by association.

However, let me be clear: I completely disagree with the premise that credibility is like virginity. You can regain your credibility if you choose to.

Regaining your credibility will be difficult and time consuming, but it can be done. If you take responsibility for your actions and your future and incorporate the right strategy, you can establish your own personal credibility and leave the stigma of the previous association behind.

Start by Taking Responsibility

It begins with the statement made by Brian Koslow at the beginning of this chapter. It must start by taking responsibility for your actions. If you simply throw your hands in the air and give up simply because of the reputation you've inherited due to the actions of your predecessors, you'll never establish real credibility in the marketplace. If, on the other hand, you truly accept the fact that building, establishing and maintaining your credibility is your personal responsibility, you can, in fact, make it happen.

In the chapters to follow, I will outline specific steps you can take to establish your own identity and credibility. While I go into much more detail later, let me highlight some key points about what it is going to take to establish real credibility in the marketplace.

Follow Through

The biggest challenge for all sales professionals is found in the habit of follow through. Too often sales professionals make promises to return with more information, or get answers to critical questions or to address issues and problems and then they disappear. Unless the customer calls to follow up themselves, the answers never come.

Following through with commitments to your customers is the number one rule for establishing credibility. Follow through is what separates the real professionals from the wanabees. It tells customers that you are a person of your word and that you truly care.

Thought Leadership

One of the biggest complaints customers have is that the only time they see their sales rep is when the rep wants to sell something. This is a tremendous blow to the credibility of the sales professional. To offset this, you must position yourself as a Thought Leader in your marketplace.

What is a Thought Leader? Thought Leaders are the informed opinion leaders and the go-to people in their field of expertise. They are trusted sources who move and inspire people with innovative ideas; turn ideas into reality, and know and show how to replicate their success.

Thought Leaders provide ideas and strategies that help their customers. When they visit, they are best known for the ideas they leave behind or the assistance they provide. As a result, when customers have questions about their business or needs they have, they reach out first to the thought leader regardless if that is his area of expertise or not. The bottom line is that thought leaders are trusted, respected and highly thought of.

Establish Credibility Through a Web Presence

We operate in a world where the buyer is far more educated than ever before. The World Wide Web provides so much information that customers are able to identify, select and make their buying decision before every contacting a sales professional. While this can create other complications because of so much misinformation on the internet, the reality is people tend to believe what they see, hear and read on the internet.

A great way to establish initial credibility is to create a strong web presence. Whether you are an individual sales professional or a business, regardless you must establish online credibility through a web presence. Some of the ways to do this that I will discuss further in a subsequent chapter include:

- Establish an internet domain name using your own name
- Create your own website
- Start blogging
- Get active on social media for business purposes

Each of these, done properly and consistently, will establish an internet presence that will build your online credibility. All a customer has to do is Google your name and, based on the results, your credibility can be initially established in nanoseconds.

If you are truly committed to dominating your market, developing and nurturing your credibility is an important step in the process.

Chapter Six

Email Marketing Strategies

The use of an effective email marketing strategy can have a significant impact on your ability to develop a market domination strategy. Email marketing has replaced the way information is shared. The process is inexpensive, easy to create and can help you reach a wide range of people with well-timed and effectively targeted messages.

My favorite strategy is the use of email newsletters or e-Newsletters for short. The e-Newsletter is ideal for providing a consistent theme and a compilation of value-added information that your readers will find useful. This process is fairly easy to create and implement, however the key is found in your consistency and commitment to using it.

When people tell me they've had little to no success using email marketing, I typically find that they are guilty of abusing the process. What this means is that they have crossed the line from being an information source – the ultimate Thought Leader – and have, instead, leapt on to the bandwagon with all the others who are sending email blasts simply hawking products and/or services. When the focus of your content is on blatant, obvious marketing messages, you suddenly become part of the noise irritating the ears (or eyes in this case) of your readers. For every single value-based, information-based email, your readers receive at least fifty, maybe more, marketing messages that are designed to do nothing but sell. And the first impulse when the aggravation builds? Unsubscribe!

Your goal is to create a network of readers who actually look forward to seeing your e-Newsletters. To accomplish this, you need to provide:

- Ideas that will boost or help their business
- Information about benchmarks in their respective industry
- New or different ways your services or products are making a difference

Is Your Message Relevant?

The key to your success is to ensure your e-Newsletter is relevant. What do I mean by relevant? Well, let's start by understanding the definition of relevant. According the Merriam-Webster dictionary, it means:

- having significant and demonstrable bearing on the matter at hand
- affording evidence tending to prove or disprove the matter at issue or under discussion <*relevant* testimony >
- having social relevance

So before you hit "send" on your e-Newsletter campaign, ask yourself if your content is truly relevant:

- Am I attempting to sell anything in this email?
  - If so, stop and completely rewrite your email.
- Does this email provide ideas that can potentially assist most any business?
  - If yes, you're good to go.

- Is my email outside the box because it provides a social message or theme relevant to your community or a specific cause?
  - Again, if yes, you're good to go.

Sending relevant content that is both readable and usable is the first master step in creating lasting and growing email campaigns. If you can truly master this step, you're on the path to establishing yourself as a real Thought Leader.

I'm not a Writer

I understand; not everyone considers themselves to be a great writer, but everyone is a writer at some level. Whether you write correspondence or proposals, it requires you to write. Yes, you may argue that there may be a difference and you, in fact, really aren't much of a writer. I want you to understand that there are a couple of ways to get around this.

The first step is to stay fully engaged in the project and leverage the massive amount of great information available to you on the internet. There are great resources that you can use to simplify your process while remaining relevant to your audience.

Just think of all the magazines and publications that support businesses worldwide:

- ✓ Forbes
- ✓ Business Week
- ✓ The Wall Street Journal
- ✓ Inc. Magazine
- ✓ Entrepreneur Magazine
- ✓ Wired Magazine
- ✓ The Business Journal

I could go on, but I think you get the idea. Each of these publications contain well written articles with insightful information ready to be used. And with just a few key strokes, you can instantly share this information with your readers.

To do so, find an article that you believe will be of interest to most, if not all, of your readers. Copy the headline of the article into the headline spot on the e-Newsletter. Next, provide the name of the author as well as the date of publication. After you've done this, copy the first paragraph or two and paste it into the email. Finally, create text at the bottom of the post that reads, "To continue reading..." and create a hyperlink using the web address for the article. And you're done!

The other option you can use is to hire this work out. There are thousands of people available worldwide who are available to work on a time-based or project-base basis. Some of the options available can be found here:

- ❖ www.elance.com/hire-writers
- ❖ www.contentwriters.com
- ❖ www.coworks.com

The cost can vary from $7 per hour to $20 per hour or more. The key is to get samples of their work to review and then send them an assignment as a test. The investment is minimal to have someone prove their worth in order to get quality content.

Once you've found the right person, simply give them the assignment and let them go to work. This frees you up to do other important tasks. When they send you the content, simply cut and paste it into the email format and you're off and running.

Choosing an Email Service

Back in the '90s, well before internet services were available to provide the kind of email marketing services I do now, I used pretty rudimentary processes. Using my CRM software (at that time Act! was my software of choice), I would create email campaigns, select my email list and hit send. Within an hour or so, I would begin to get hounded by various people in the organization who knew what I was doing. Because my campaign went directly through our email server, it hogged all the bandwidth which, at that time, was a scarce commodity. Eventually I found a way to time my outgoing campaigns so they went out when it wouldn't impact anyone else.

Then I was introduced to a variety of internet-based email subscription services. Some of the best include:

- ConstantContact.com
- aWeber.com
- Mailchimp.com

47

- Verticalresponse.com
- Infusionsoft.com

Some are more expensive than others, while some are easier and more robust than others. You simply need to do some research to find the one that works best for you. Most will let you start with a 30-day trial allowing you to import a small number of addresses in order to test the service out. I'd recommend doing the trial in order to get a better understanding of the service, its ease of use and its overall functionality.

Before choosing an email service, here are a few things to consider:

- **Reporting Tools** – Make sure the service offers comprehensive reporting tools. This includes a list of who opened your emails, who clicked on a link you provided, who opted out or didn't receive their email, etc. These are very powerful in helping you follow up on the reader activity.

- **Subscription Option** – Choose a service that provides a way to allow interested individuals to subscribe to your distribution list. Do they provide a connection to social media tools such as Facebook to help your followers sign up? Do they provide the tools to create a "sign up" button for your website?

- **Easy to Use Templates** – Nothing aggravates me more than hard-to-use email templates. Investigate the quality and ease-of-use of the templates provided by the service.

- **Social Media Marketing** – In recent years, many email marketing services recognized the unfulfilled need to provide a service that helped provide social media marketing services. Constant Contact, for example, provides the tools to create Facebook promotion landing pages that draw potential fans in. Leveraging Facebook and your email list, you can market your page and gain more fans. If you're interested in building your following on Facebook, make sure you have access to this tool or something similar.

- **Surveys** – One option to look for is the ability to create surveys. This can be an invaluable tool to use. While there are survey sites, such as Survey Monkey, out there to use, why not combine your tools under one umbrella?

- **Event Marketing Tools** – Another is the ability to create an email campaign for an upcoming event and have access to a landing page for those who want more information as well as a way to provide RSVP assistance so they can register for the event with minimal effort.

How Often Should I Publish?

This is a great question. I get asked this a lot and there is a divided opinion on the matter. There are those who are concerned with bombarding the subscription list with too many emails. What if they get upset and want to unsubscribe?

Let me answer the question with my opinion. Granted, this is simply my personal opinion based on over 25 years of doing a wide range of email marketing campaigns, but still it's just my opinion.

To be frank, I recommend emailing them as often as you can. If you blog and connect your blog to your email service, you can set it to distribute an email campaign every time you post a blog. You can create a drip campaign that will send out a different, but similar message every day if you desire.

Yes, your audience gets a lot of email, but yours are going to be different. How?

- ✓ The content is going to be relevant
- ✓ It will arrive consistently
- ✓ It will be high quality

I've already addressed the issue of relevancy, so let me discuss the other two points.

Set your calendar up with recurring activities for the creation of and distribution of your e-Newsletter. If you want to do this once a week, set it up accordingly. Select the day and time and stay consistent with it. If you want to send it three times a week or once a month, just be consistent – same days, same time, all the time.

Lastly, don't skimp on quality. Your e-Newsletter is YOU when you're not there. While that sounds odd, consider the fact that regardless of where you are, when your e-Newsletter goes out, it's as if you're making hundreds, if not thousands, of sales calls simultaneously. You wouldn't go on a sales call in your sweats or pajamas, would you? You'd brush your teeth and do your hair first, right? The same is true of your email marketing campaigns. They must be high quality. They must be impeccable. Make sure you spellcheck your work and then spellcheck it another time. Make sure every link in your email works and goes to the correct source.

Regarding double checking every web link in your email before sending your campaign out, let me leave you with this thought. Ever hear about the teacher who wanted to show her elementary school students the White House's website as a part of the learning experience? This was in the early days of the internet, when schools were first implementing computers and the web as a learning experience. She set up her students in the computer lab and had them type in the web address: www.whitehouse.com. At that time, this website was a porn site. A simple change from .com to .org and the problem is averted. Let's just say it was an eye-opening experience for the students and very embarrassing situation for the teacher. Don't make the same mistake in your email.

Chapter Seven

Blog to Build Your Brand

According to statistics from Wordpress, a very well-known hosting site for bloggers, the statistics for blogging are quite staggering:

- ✓ 33.9 million new blogs are created every month
- ✓ Bloggers produce approximately 60.1 million new posts each month
- ✓ Over 61.5 million new comments are made on blogs every month
- ✓ Over 409 million people view more than 19.1 billion pages each month

Additionally, there are those who have created a small fortune as a result of the success of their blogging efforts. Here is the list of the top 10 blog earners in 2013 according to the ***www.therichest.com*** website:

#10: Ewdison Then – "SlashGear": $60,000 to $80,000 per month

#9: Matt Marshall – "VentureBeat": $50,000 to $100,000 per month

#8: Gina Trapani – "Lifehacker": $110,000 per month

#7: Collis Ta'eed – "TutsPlus": $55,000 to $120,000 per month

#6: Jake Dobki – "Gothamist": $80,000 to $110,000 per month

#5: Timothy Sykes – "TimothySykes.com ": $150,000 to $180,000 per month

#4: Vitaly Friedman – "SmashingMagazine": $150,000 to $190,000 per month

#3: Mario Lavanderia – "Perez Hilton": $200,000 to $400,000 per month

#2: Pete Cashmore – "Mashable": $560,000 to $600,000 per month

#1: Michael Arrington – "TechCrunch": $500,000 to $800,000 per month

I share this information simply to show you the strength of blogging and all that it can do. Blogging provides individuals as well as companies access to a worldwide audience who are seeking to connect with specific interests and expertise. As a result of the credibility developed over time, the list of the top ten income earning blogs is representative of the financial rewards as well.

What is a blog?

In short, blogs are short articles containing content about specific subject matter. Some blog sites discuss a wide variety of topics while the most successful blogs focus on specific topics. The list above represents a few different industries, but most are in the technology field. Blogs literally run the gamut from sewing information to cooking to fast cars. The most important point, however, is that the most successful blogs are short, to the point and interesting, if not also entertaining.

Why You Need a Blog

Blogging is a great way to develop individual credibility and establish your reputation as a Thought Leader. While a blog doesn't have to be complex or very deep in content, it does need to provide relevant content that people can use and refer to.

When you blog, you gain more traction on Google searches than a traditional website. While traditional websites for too many companies tend to be static – meaning the content doesn't change much at all – blogs, on the other hand, are changing all the time. Whether you blog daily, weekly or sporadically, new content gets added. The simple act of adding new content has a significant weight with the new search engine optimization metrics now employed by Google.

How Do I Learn to Blog?

One of the best ways to learn to blog is to follow other bloggers. As simple as that sounds, it is extremely effective and powerful. On the blogosphere, there are many successful blogs that you can learn quite a bit from simply by reading their posts. Hee are some examples:

- 10 Blogs Every Entrepreneur Should Follow
  - Mashable
  - Fast Company
  - Forbes: Entrepreneurs
  - TechCrunch
  - VentureBeat
  - You're the Boss
  - LinkedIn Today
  - Chris Brogran
  - Duct Tape Marketing
  - Marketing Profs: Small Business

- Additional Blogs to Consider
  - Seth Godin
  - Jeffrey Gittomer
  - Salesforce
  - Jill Konrath
  - Hubspot
  - Tom Hackelman (my personal favorite)

Some Practical Tips for Blogging

1. **Don't Start Out by Paying to Blog.** There are a number of blogging choices; some charge a monthly hosting fee while others arc frcc. I recommend you subscribe to free services such as Blogger.com or Wordpress.

   The advantage of Blogger is that the service is owned by Google. Like all of us, Google likes most of all to promote material that drives people to their platforms. As a result, it's very easy for a blog on Blogger to get found.

The thing I like about Wordpress is you can literally kill three birds in one. Earlier in my book I challenge you to create your own domain name and start a personal website. Wordpress will help you do both while also serving as the host for your blog – all at the same time. The nice thing is the cost to purchase the domain name is very inexpensive and, unless you want a lot of extra features, that's about all you pay for.

2. **Post Often.** The best read blogs are blogs that are posted often. Seth Godin, who I follow, is the master of this. Seth is known for posting three or four posts per day. They're short and sweet and are typically insightful and also entertaining. Also, the more you post and the more consistently that you post, the more likely that the search engines will point readers towards your blog.

3. **Leverage Your Smartphone.**
Blogger and Wordpress both offer apps for the iOS and Android operating systems. This enables you to blog throughout the day regardless if you have your computer with you or not.

4. **Post Comments on Other Blogs.**
When you read someone's blog post, add a comment to it with a reference back to your own blog. The search engines like this a lot and it will help bring greater awareness to your blog.

5. **Focus Your Blog on a Specific Niche.** The worst thing you can do is to create a blog that is so random that no one can clearly state what your purpose is in one short, succinct statement. If it's about marketing ideas, post about marketing. If it's about cars, post about cars and car-related information. The narrower, more focused your niche, the more successful your blog will be.

6. **Ask other bloggers to post a blog about something you write.** If you were to get Seth Godin, for example, to post a response or comment about something on your blog, you will reach a whole new stratosphere, at

least for a time. Successful bloggers attract a large audience and the best thing you can do is to tap into their success if you can.

7. **Read books about blogging.** There is a wide range of books on the subject and it's a continually evolving topic as people get a better grasp of the power of blogging, so check out it out at your local bookstore.

8. **Hire Your Writing Out if Necessary.** As I point out in the chapter on email marketing, there are a large number of resources available to help write content for your blog. Start with the sources I shared and Google for more options.

Blogging is a very powerful tool for building credibility and becoming known as the "go-to" person in your local market place. Leverage this tool as much as you can.

Chapter Eight

The Power of White Papers and Free Reports

Another powerful tool for developing a credible reputation as the local industry expert and get person talking about you is to provide timely and well-written white papers and free reports. When free reports and white papers are provided to potential clients with relevant and timely information, your reputation is strengthened making it easier to open doors to new account opportunities.

The best use of a white paper or free report is to help you accumulate data about potential interested prospects. Individuals are more likely to provide you with their contact information, such as their email address, when you offer a free report in exchange. This not only helps strengthen your credibility, but also helps build your database.

What's the Difference Between a White Paper and a Free Report?

Let's start by discussing the "Free Report." The free report is designed to be short and to the point. It is written about a concise topic and typically will be about three to five pages at the very most. With a free report, brevity is critical. Your intent is to whet the appetite of your potential clients enough that they want to learn more.

A white paper, on the other hand, provides a more detailed introduction to a key subject. While it can be short like a free report, often the reader desires a white paper for its more detailed insights into the subject at hand. At the same time, however, a white paper is also leveraged to entice the reader to learn just enough that they come to you for more information.

Here are some great tips to consider:

1. **Choose a topic that your audience will be interested in.** I know; this is beginning to sound like a broken record, but it's like the old marketing adage: Location, location, location. Choose a topic that many, if not all, in your target audience will want to seek out.

2. **Keep it short, but not too short.** If it's a couple of pages or less, just put it in your blog. Business people want helpful information, so provide it for them. But don't overwhelm them with too much information. Finding the right balance is an art form, so practice.

3. **Use it as a free tool that will help you gather information.** One of the biggest challenges for

salespeople is gathering information about prospective clients. Using the "Free Report" that has a title that will get their attention is a great way to navigate them to your website. When they visit your website to get the free report, the only "cost" is they are asked to fill out a very short form that will provide you with data you might not have received otherwise. It's amazing how much information people will give in order to get a free report that they're interested in.

4. **Follow up.** After they download the report, follow up to discuss the practical applications of the report. If you can schedule a phone meeting, or better yet, a face-to-face meeting, it strengthens the power of your report and your client's view of you and positions you for a business opportunity.

Consider the various topics your target audience will be interested in. What topics can you provide information about that lead to further interest in your products or service? Identifying several ideas will provide you with the starting point for creating your special reports.

Chapter Nine

The Power of Public Speaking

"According to most studies, people's number one fear is public speaking. Number two is death. Death is number two. Does that sound right? This means to the average person, if you go to a funeral, you're better off in the casket than delivering the eulogy." – Jerry Seinfeld

"All of us are born with a set of instinctive fears, of falling, of the dark, of lobsters, of falling on lobsters in the dark, or speaking before the Rotary Club, or the words 'some assembly required.'" – Dave Barry

"Feel the fear of public speaking and do it anyway." – Arvee Robinson

I find it incredibly entertaining to see gifted, successful sales professional melt when asked to speak publically. They begin to tremble and get tongue tied. They literally break out into a sweat. These are men and women who speak for a living, but they fall faint when given the opportunity to present to a group larger than twenty-five people.

Public speaking is one of the most important things you can ever do in your career. Not only does it provide you with confidence to speak in front of others regardless the size of the crowd, but it helps build your product and/or industry knowledge. As you have likely heard before, those who teach learn the most. In order to be effective and provide an insightful, well thought out message, you will invest the time necessary to be fully comfortable with your message. As a result, this drills the material even further down into your mind that it becomes second nature.

The following are some excerpts from a Forbes Magazine article entitled, **How Warren Buffett and Joel Osteen Conquered their Terrifying Fear of Public Speaking**, written by Carmine Gallo.

Billionaire investor Warren Buffett was "terrified" of public speaking. He was so nervous, in fact, that he would arrange and choose his college classes to avoid having to get up in front of people. He even enrolled in a public speaking course and dropped out before it even started. "I lost my nerve," he said. At the age of 21, Buffett started his career in the securities business in Omaha and decided that to reach his full potential, he had to overcome his fear of public speaking.

Buffett enrolled in a Dale Carnegie course with another thirty people who, like him, were "terrified of getting up and saying our names." Buffett revealed his early insecurity in this interview for Levo League, a career website for young women. The host asked Buffett, "What habits did you cultivate in your 20s and 30s that you

see as the foundation of success?"
Buffett answered, " You've got to be
able to communicate in life and it's
enormously important. Schools, to
some extent, under emphasize that. If
you can't communicate and talk to
other people and get across your
ideas, you're giving up your potential."

…The world famous minister, Joel
Osteen, sells out places like Yankee
Stadium and speaks live to 40,000 a
week who visit Lakewood church
every Sunday (the mega-church
meets in Houston at the former
Compaq Center). Osteen says the
week before his first sermon in 1999
marked the worst days of his life. "I
was scared to death," he says. At the
time he knew very little about speaking
or preparing a message. In fact he
was perfectly content to sit behind the
video camera during his father's
sermons. When his father passed
away, Osteen's wife and family
encouraged him to take the stage.

Joel Osteen did not overcome his
fear for a long time. The conversations
he heard didn't help. "I overheard two
ladies say, 'he's not as good as his
father.' I was already insecure and—
boom—another negative label."
Words, he says, are like seeds. If you
dwell on them long enough they take
root and you will become what those
words say you'll become—if you let
them. Osteen says negative labels—

the ones people place on us and the labels we place on ourselves—prevent us from reaching our potential.

Gallo goes on to share three important points regarding how to overcome your fear of public speaking:

1. **Manage Your Fear** – "Successful public speakers learn to manage their fear and not to eliminate it."

2. **Reframe Your Thoughts** – "You can't control what other people say about you…but you can control how you frame those comments and you can most certainly control the things you tell yourself." Focus on affirming yourself rather than concentrating on the negative.

3. **Do What You Fear. A Lot.** – "Enrolling in a public-speaking course was a good first step to helping Buffett build his confidence as a public speaker. The key, he said, was signing up to teach a night course at the University of Nebraska—Omaha. Buffett taught investment principles to students twice his age. He did it to force himself to stand up and talk to people. Once Osteen decided to be the new pastor of Lakewood, he was

forced to preach every week. Both Buffett and Osteen improved their public speaking skills over time because they did it over and over again."

Here are a few tips and ideas for you to consider:

1. **Register in a course to help develop your speaking skills.** Warren Buffett did this by registering for and attending a Dale Carnegie course. Your local community college will often have courses available to help in this area as well. Another option, if it's available, is to get involved with a local Toastmasters chapter.

2. **Start getting good practice by simply making yourself available.** There are so many ways you can get the practice in front of audiences who will listen, participate, but you won't lose any business at the same time. High school teachers are always looking for special speakers to present ideas or career information to their students.

3. **Get involved in the speaker's bureau in your community.** The chamber of commerce in your community typically has a "speaker's bureau" that you can participate in. Simply let them know what topics you are able to

speak about and make yourself available.

4. **Offer your expertise to the local Rotary, Lions Club and other civic clubs.** This is a great way to get connected, plugged in and well-known.

5. **Use the subjects you're already using.** Go back to your e-Newsletter, your blog and your free reports as the sources of ideas for sharing in your presentations.

6. **Offer your free report or copies of your PowerPoint slides to attendees in exchange for their business card.** This always gets you a good share of business cards from the attendees and a solid list of suspects for your business.

7. **Be informative, not "salesy."** This is your opportunity to position yourself as the subject matter expert, not just another salesperson. By focusing on an informative, educational topic, you will get your point across while also showing that you are someone who is trustworthy and capable.

Chapter Ten

Seminar Events

Another way to build your reputation as a Thought Leader is to host regular seminars events. Seminars provide a forum where you can provide specific content, focused on a specific segment of the market that provides ideas and educational content.

Think about this for a minute: You've heard of special speakers hosting free events before, haven't you? I've been to these before where a star-studded lineup was on hand to present. There were six speakers for the day, each with 45 minutes to an hour to speak. Each speaker was a motivational and training expert including Zig Ziglar, Tom Hopkins, Brian Tracy and others. They each provided valuable content and no sales pitch was made.

The catch? There wasn't one.

As long as you didn't walk out into the hallway to use the restroom or make a phone call.

In the hallway, there were kiosks lined up representing each individual speaker at the event. Their books, videos and CDs were available to purchase and real sales pros were at these kiosks ready to sell the speaker's goods and training services. And trust me, after hearing just one of the speakers, even I was out there buying what I could to help reinforce what I had just learned.

This is what the seminar event is for you. It is an opportunity to provide valuable, relevant material to your current as well as prospective clients. There is no sales pitch. Instead the focus is solely on providing ideas that are going to help those who attend.

One of the best benefits for me in providing these types of events is that people truly appreciate it. Whether it's something as simple as a Lunch & Learn or an all-day seminar, clients appreciate the effort you make to provide valuable, insightful information. And if you continue to do this on a regular, consistent basis, your clients will be after you to let them know when the next one is planned.

Workshop tips for success:

1. **Keep your focus narrow and concise.** Nothing is worse than attending a workshop that is too long and travels in too many directions. Have a short time frame and focus on one specific topic and your attendees will be very appreciative.

2. **Promote, promote, promote.** Make everyone aware of your event using all tools available to you. Personally, face-to-face, invite every desired guest and then continue to follow up. The day before the event, follow up with everyone to remind and encourage them to attend.

3. **Invite other "experts" to join you in presenting.** Since it's your workshop, make sure you are very clear about the expectation, the available time frame, and how you need them to participate.

4. **Pay for the event by inviting resources who will potentially benefit from the workshop to participate.** If their company can be used as a resource to help support the topic you are presenting, invite them to be a host for a small fee. Invite enough and the cost of your event can potentially be cost-free.

5. **Follow up.** In the days immediately following your workshop, personally visit every account and follow up. What was one idea they came away with? How will they use it? What can you do to support them in taking action?

6. **Ask for feedback.** As your workshop draws to a close, ask everyone to provide some written information about what they learned, what they might want to learn more about, and what you

can do differently in the future to provide the very best workshop. Give away a free the drawing mechanism.

You may be surprised at the level of work it takes to pull off a successful seminar event. The first one or two will require the most work simply because this is your first time to do such an event. But the rewards are great.

One word of advice: Don't skimp on the effort; it will show up at your event. In particular, put a significant amount of effort into encouraging people to attend. Beg, plead, if necessary. Assure them that they will leave the event with at least one solid idea that they can take action on immediately. And then deliver!

Chapter Eleven

The Power of Social Media Marketing

Unless you've been living on a secluded island for the past twenty years, you are well aware of the phenomenon of social media. From the early days of MySpace to Facebook and others, social media has dramatically changed the face of business as well as the world.

The Impact of Social Media

Here are some insightful numbers regarding the usage of social media platforms in 2014 from AdWeek:

- **Facebook**
  - 1.28 billion monthly active users
  - There are over 1 billion mobile monthly active users
  - 72% of online adults visit Facebook at least once a month
  - 75% of the engagement on a post happens in the first five hours
- **Google+**
  - 540 million monthly active users and 1.6 billion subscribed users

- 22% of online adults visit Google+ once a month
- 53% of interaction between a Google+ user and Brand is positive

- **Twitter**
  - 255 million monthly active users with over 1 billion total subscribed users
  - 78% of Twitter's active users are mobile
  - 46% of users tweet at least once per day

- **Instagram**
  - 200 million monthly active users and the subscription base continues to grow at an exponential rate
  - 23% of teens consider Instagram as their favorite social network
  - 50 million users signed up to Instagram in the last six months

- **LinkedIn**
  - 187 million monthly active users with over 300 million subscribers
  - More than 2 users sign-up for LinkedIn every second
  - LinkedIn reaches a total of 200 countries and territories
  - 44,000: The average number of daily LinkedIn mobile job applications that are submitted

- **Pinterest**
  - 40 million monthly active uses and 70 million total users
  - 80% of Pinterest users are female
  - 158 is the average number of pins from female users
  - 84% of women and 50% of men stay active on Pinterest
  - 23% of users use it at least once a day

- **YouTube**
  - 1 billion total users
  - 80% of traffic is from outside the United States
  - 6 billion hours of video is watched on YouTube every month
  - 100 hours of video is uploaded on YouTube per minute
  - 1 billion is the average YouTube mobile video views per day

Is There Real Value to Me?

If these staggering numbers are not enough to convince you of the broad marketing opportunity available to you on social media, I may have difficulty converting you. But I'll try.

What is the goal of my book and the purpose for which you are reading? To shift from obscurity to market domination, correct? To accomplish this, if you use few, if any, of the strategies contained in my book, I challenge you to leverage social media to your advantage.

Here's why: Social media empowers you to specifically target, almost like a laser beam, your niche market. If you are seeking business men and women, ages 30 to 50, who are midlevel management or above, social media can help you get your message to these people. Whatever your specific target looks like, social media has eyes on the target already; all you have to do is take action.

For example, today I ran a one-day Facebook campaign for my book, Roar Like You Mean It! and, based on my metrics, my ad is expected to get exposed to between 95,000 and 170,000 people in a 24 hour period. My cost was minimal but my target precise and my message powerful.

But I Prefer to Keep My Business Life Separate from My Private Life

I know and I really do understand, but you also need to understand that men in Hell want water. If you are going to be successful and, more importantly, dominate your market, you need to get off your backside and leverage the tools you've been given.

The days of keeping business and home life separate are gone. So is the middle class. You can either continue to slide backward and lose market share or you can begin to take your career seriously and make a difference.

People do business with people who:

- ✓ They connect with
- ✓ The message is relevant

✓ Are people first, business second
✓ Have flaws
✓ Are human

This is why you cannot segregate your business life from your personal life. You must actively participate, be real, and show that you have a human side.

Tips to Utilizing Social Media

The following tips outline some specific things you can do using my recommended social media channels. I also recommend that you invest some time reading more about these tools and finding what others have to say.

- **Set up a LinkedIn account immediately.** To get a better idea about what a good, solid LinkedIn page should look like, please go to my page and view my profile. Simply type in "Tom Hackelman" into the search bar and view my page. After you sign up, connect with me so we can share contacts.

- **Leverage your existing contacts within LinkedIn.** Allow LinkedIn to search your address book to see who is already on LinkedIn that you know. With Outlook, simply download a .csv file of all your contacts and then import them into LinkedIn. With Gmail, LinkedIn will connect automatically as soon as you authorize it. Doing this will enable you to reach out to each of your contacts who are already on LinkedIn and invite them to connect. Often you will find that potential clients that you've been chasing are on LinkedIn and now you can connect and strengthen the relationship.

- **Provide recommendations for your associates and customers on LinkedIn.** Again, what you are doing is providing value to them by stating how you feel about their work and their service. In return, most people will do the same for you. I cut and paste the recommendations I receive onto a Word document that I can share with potential clients to show what others are saying about me.

- **Write and publish blog posts on LinkedIn.** This is one of the newer features on LinkedIn and I love it. I can take a blog I've already written on my personal site and cut and paste it to LinkedIn. Once there, it receives a broad audience. You will be able to visit the post and see how many people have read it, liked it, and see how many comments were made.

- **Download and use the LinkedIn Connected app on your smartphone.** This is a great new app that feeds information about updates on every one of your LinkedIn connections. For example, I check it every morning and it lets me know who has a birthday, a business anniversary, and those who changed jobs. I can then send a brief note of congratulations to each. Doing this every day takes just a few minutes but also keeps you up-to-date with each of your connections.

- **Create a Facebook page.** If you already have one, let's review some ground rules. Most people have traditionally used it for "personal" reasons and have party pics and funny stories posted on their page. The problem is — do you really want that potential $1 million contract to fade away just because your contact saw the pictures on Facebook of you staggering drunk? Didn't think so! Do your best to keep it relatively clean, but also keep it human. Simply use good judgment recognizing that what gets posted to the internet, regardless of the tool, it's there forever. You'll thank me later!

- **To build your Facebook connections, you can do the same for Facebook as you can for LinkedIn in terms of connecting with people in your database.** You will find some are on Facebook but not LinkedIn; this way you reach a wider audience.

- **Reach out to your Facebook connections every time it's their birthday.** Facebook will keep you posted on when each person's birthday is occurring. Just go to their page and add a quick "Happy Birthday!" to their front page and you'll be sure to get a major thank you for remembering them on their birthday.

- **Set up your Twitter account.** Twitter and Facebook will both connect with your blog, if you have a blog set up. Every time I blog, my Twitter and Facebook statuses are immediately updated with the title of my blog post and a link to the post. Assuming you write valuable, interesting content, your readership of your blog will continue to increase.

- **Don't beg or pay for Twitter followers!** There are a lot of trolls on Twitter who claim to be able to provide you with thousands of new followers. Don't get caught in the scam. While I recognize that there are some valid services out there, I suggest you look at the follower count of those promoting this service. One recent troll reached out offering to increase my follower count and when I looked at the numbers, I found they had a staggering 320 (tongue in cheek) followers. The bottom line is, if this actually worked everyone would be doing it and the real value of Twitter would diminish. The true value of Twitter and the growth of your follower base comes by providing valuable content and insight. When you do this, the followers show up.

- **Stay active.** Social media marketing is only effective when it is used regularly. I don't spend

80

hours upon hours online using social media. I update information early in the morning and then check it in the evening. At the same time, however, there are a number of services, Hootsuite, for example, that you can subscribe to that will help you stay active without having to do a lot of the heavy lifting. By connecting your Twitter and Facebook accounts to Hootsuite, you can create a number of messages that will be sent out at specific times throughout the day. It's just another way of maximizing your time and getting the biggest bang for the buck.

Let me close this chapter about social media marketing by sharing one of the best and most valuable reasons for being involved: Web presence. The three social media tools that I have shared with you are at the top of the Google food chain. When you Google yourself and you find little to nothing about yourself in the results, a large reason can be found in your absence from or lack of activity on social media.

Lastly, by creating such a powerful presence on the web, you will find opportunities for both clients and job opportunities. When potential clients search Google for your particular product or service, they will find you popping up everywhere when you use social media effectively. When a headhunter is looking for top flight sales champion in your industry to interview for a Fortune

500 company, how strong will your name appear when they start their search? Social media works in many, many ways. Just don't ignore it; use it!

Section Three

Creating an Action Plan
for Market Domination

Chapter Twelve

Creating the Action Plan

"First comes thought; then organization of that thought, into ideas and plans; then transformation of those plans into reality. The beginning, as you will observe, is in your imagination."

--Napoleon Hill

"He, who every morning plans the transactions of the day, and follows that plan, carries a thread that will guide him through a labyrinth of the most busy life."

--Victor Hugo

Through this book, I have covered quite a bit of ground about ways to dominate your market. The question now is this: Are you truly committed to do whatever it takes to dominate your market? Do you really want to take the next steps and begin the process of dominating your market? If so, Section Three is for you.

It begins with a plan. All great accomplishments in life began as a dream that was written down as a goal and then an action plan was created. Then the action plan was put into motion. That is the creation process. All of creation occurs twice; it begins first in the mind and then in the actions we take to make it a reality.

Dominating your market space begins first with clearly articulating your dreams and desires and then creating an action plan to accomplish them. If you are truly ready to get started, the following steps will help you accomplish this.

Where Are You Today?

To start, let's identify where you are today. You need to be honest about where you really are if you are going to make serious progress in the right direction. The following questions are going to ask you to get real clear about where you, your business and your competition are at, to the best of your ability, today.

If you are a sales professional, I want you to address the following questions recognizing that you are, in fact, a small business. While you may sell for and work for a specific company and they provide the inventory, support, billing, and service for the products and/or services you sell, you are the "owner" of your territory. Your territory and all that is contained in it is, in fact, your small business.

If you would like to receive a free digital version of the following document, please email me at tom@thomashackelman.com to request it at no charge.

About You

What products and/or services do you sell?	
What is your value proposition?	
Describe your ideal customer	
What is your revenue plan for this fiscal year? (or upcoming year)	

What is your actual performance year-to-date	
% of plan	
List each of the past three years (i.e., 20014, 2013, and 2012) and report the final revenue numbers for each	
Are your numbers improving, declining, or staying the same?	
What are your company's strengths?	
What are your company's weaknesses?	

What opportunities exist for your business to grow and expand?	
What threats exist for or to your business?	
To the best of your knowledge, what is your current market share?	
Where does your market share need to be to be considered the dominant player?	

About Your Competition

List all of your primary competitors	
Who is the top competitor in your market space?	
Who is your second leading competitor?	
What is the value proposition of each of these two?	

What strengths do each bring to the market?	
What specific weaknesses do each have?	

How do they currently market themselves? (consider everything – advertising, social media, sales activities, etc.)	
What is the value proposition for each?	

To the best of your knowledge, what is the market share percentage for each?	

Pre-Planning

What specific sales-related activities do your top two competitors NOT do?	
Of their sales related activities, in what areas do you need to exceed them? (i.e., # of calls, # of appointments, etc.)	

What tools do they not use? (i.e., Facebook, blogging, email campaigns, etc.)	
What do their sales professionals look like? (i.e., from an appearance standpoint, do they dress casual, high dollar, etc.)	

Now that you have a concise and clear view of where you and your key competitors are at, it's time to create some specific goals for yourself. As we go through this next step in the process, remember that dominating requires establishing goals for yourself that are going to truly stretch you to a much higher level. If your income goal is $100,000 per year presently, what would happen if you decided to raise it 5x or 10x? Is that high? You bet it is! But if we don't raise our own expectations of ourselves, who will?

Raise your expectations, both in terms of your goals as well as in terms of what you are prepared to do to accomplish them. No one else will do it for you. In fact, they will likely root against you or advise you to lower your expectations to avoid "disappointment." Let them continue to swim in mediocrity and raise your expectations of yourself.

My Goals

My income goal:	
How I want to impact the world or contribute to make a difference	
What do I want for my family?	
"Toys" I want to acquire	
Describe what your life will look like in five years	

Describe what your life will look like in ten years	

Your Market Domination Game Plan

Next we are going to create your personal market domination game plan. As you complete this step, you will be asked to make some decisions on different tools and strategies you will use. I am not recommending that you use each and every one of these; that will drive you crazy. Instead I want you to select the key strategies you will commit to and then take action on these strategies consistently and persistently each and every day. Each of these are going to stretch you and, at first, it's not going to feel natural. That's normal. But commit to doing this for twenty-one days straight at a minimum and you will begin to see the results.

Describe what your business is going to look like in twelve months	
How much revenue are you going to produce each month to take over your market space?	
How many new customers are you going to gain each month?	
What core activities are you committed to and to what level? **Remember, to truly dominate your space, you must take massive action.**	____ Business Development Activities ____ # of prospecting calls each day ____ # of phone calls each day ____ # of emails sent each day ____ # of handwritten cards (Thank You notes, etc.) sent each day ____ # of Appointments Each Week

	___ # of Presentations Each Week ___ # of Closes Each Week

What steps are you going to take to develop your market credibility?	___ Personal Domain
	
	    What will your domain be?
	
	___ Website
	
	___ Email Marketing Campaign
	
	    What service?
	
	    How often will you commit to sending email campaigns?
	
	___ Blogging
	
	    What blog service will you use?
	
	    How often will you commit to posting a blog?
	
	___ Seminar Events
	
	    Identify the date of your first seminar and topic:

	___ Social Media (choose a minimum of one)
	
	    ___ LinkedIn
	
	    ___ Facebook
	
	    ___ Twitter
	
	    ___ YouTube
	
	    ___ Instagram
	
	    ___ Google+
	
	    ___ Pinterest

Social Media Activity: Describe how committed you are by stating the minimum number of posts you intend to make each day	Social Media Tool:
	_____
	
	    ___ Number of posts per day
	
	Social Media Tool:
	_____
	
	    ___ Number of posts per day
	
	Social Media Tool:
	_____
	
	    ___ Number of posts per day
	
	Social Media Tool:
	_____

	___ Number of posts per day
White Papers / Free Reports	Date I will publish my first one:
Public Speaking	If training is needed, where will I receive it? When will I register and get started? List groups I can potentially speak at: List possible topics:

Next Steps

Your next steps are critical. Anthony Robbins writes:

> *"A real decision is measured*
> *By the fact that you've taken*
> *action. If there's no action,*
> *you haven't truly decided."*

You must take real action now. What you do today and each day over the next twenty-one days will impact the results you get sixty- to ninety-days from now. If your desire is to truly dominate your market space, at the end of the next quarter, you will begin to see the fruits of your labor. But it requires sowing first before you will be able to start reaping the harvest.

I want you to commit to doing what you just completed because I personally know the impact it will have on you and your business. So here are a few last things I want you to commit to:

- ✓ Every day, write your goals down. Be sure to write them down in the present tense, as if they have already happened. This will throw coals on the fire and continue to intensify your desire to make each of your goals a reality.

- ✓ Every day, write down your list of commitments you just outlined above. By writing them down each and every day, you are reminding yourself of what you've committed to do and it will encourage you to continue to take action.

- ✓ Set up recurring activities up in your calendar for the strategies you've committed to. For example, if you've committed to sending out an email campaign once a week, select the day it is to go out and what time. Set this up as a recurring activity so it's part of your calendar and treat it just like you would treat an appointment with a very important customer.

- ✓ If you need help writing content, whether for your email campaign or your white papers, start contacting people today and find someone you feel good about. And then give them their first assignment!

- ✓ Regarding social media, if you've chosen Facebook, Twitter and/or LinkedIn, set up a Hootsuite account and set this service up to help make posts for you as often as you've committed to. By setting this up in advance, you can literally let it run in an automated fashion while you are accomplishing other key tasks.

Lastly, because you are raising the stakes, there will be those who will attempt to dissuade you from your path. They will say that you're going to burn yourself out. They will try to convince you that competition is a good thing and that you should just enjoy yourself. These are the hyenas we talked about earlier. They don't understand your passion for dominating your market, so they don't understand the actions you're undertaking. This is why they live mediocre lives.

You are better than mediocre. You intend to be the best in your market space, if not in your industry. To be the best, you must begin today to act as if you've already arrived. You must take the kind of actions that will lead to market domination and keep you there. Let no one get in your way. Focus on the outcomes you desire and don't get distracted.

I leave you with this final thought from Zig Ziglar:

"You were designed for accomplishment, engineered for success, and endowed with the seeds of greatness."

I want you to live today and every day from here on with the understanding that the seeds of greatness are deep within you. With every day and with every action step you take, you are empowering these seeds to continue to grow until, almost like it's overnight, they bloom into the incredible success you were designed to be.

About Thomas Hackelman

Thomas Hackelman is a Sales Champion. He works with individuals and companies to grow their revenue, their profits and helps them design a sustainable sales culture that will continue to grow.

As the Director of Sales for Standley Systems, an Oklahoma-based and family run business technology company, Thomas has consistently grown the Southern Oklahoma Sales Region into a consistent top tier producer. He has led the majority of his team to achieve the company's annual President's Club Award as well as himself. Over the past two years alone, revenues have grown 137% and profit has grown 48%.

As a father to five children and two step-children, Thomas has proven to be a leader at home as well. All but one of his children are located across the country serving as teachers, musicians, as well as community leaders. The youngest, his step-daughter, lives at home with Thomas and her mother.

Thomas and his wife Joyce married in 2012 and reside in Norman, Oklahoma where they are huge fans of the University of Oklahoma and the Oklahoma City Thunder.

Follow Thomas Hackelman

Blog: *Serious Business Growth*
http://tomhackelman.com

Twitter:
http://twitter.com/thackelman

LinkedIn:
https://www.linkedin.com/in/tomhackelman

Facebook:
https://www.facebook.com/liongrowthstrategies

Website:
http://www.thomashackelman.com

www.ingramcontent.com/pod-product-compliance
Lightning Source LLC
Chambersburg PA
CBHW070823180526
45168CB00002B/731